TULSA CITY-COUNTY LIBRARY

skjc
7/11

S0-AEE-142

Voices of

WORLD WAR II

STORIES FROM THE FRONT LINES

by Lois Miner Huey

Consultant:
Elihu Rose
Adjunct Associate Professor
New York University
New York City, New York

CAPSTONE PRESS
a capstone imprint

Edge Books are published by Capstone Press,
151 Good Counsel Drive, P.O. Box 669, Mankato, Minnesota 56002.
www.capstonepub.com

Copyright © 2011 by Capstone Press, a Capstone imprint.
All rights reserved.
No part of this publication may be reproduced in whole or in part,
or stored in a retrieval system, or transmitted in any form or by any means,
electronic, mechanical, photocopying, recording, or otherwise, without
written permission of the publisher.
For information regarding permission, write to Capstone Press,
151 Good Counsel Drive, P.O. Box 669, Dept. R, Mankato, Minnesota 56002.

Books published by Capstone Press are manufactured with paper
containing at least 10 percent post-consumer waste.

Library of Congress Cataloging-in-Publication Data
Huey, Lois Miner.
  Voices of World War II : stories from the front lines / by Lois Miner Huey.
    p. cm.— (Edge books. Voices of war)
  Summary: "Describes first-hand accounts of World War II from those who lived
    through it"—Provided by publisher.
  Includes bibliographical references and index.
  ISBN 978-1-4296-4738-0 (library binding)
  ISBN 978-1-4296-5627-6 (paperback)
  1. World War, 1939–1945—Biography—Juvenile literature. I. Title. II. Series.
  D736.H84 2011
  940.54'8—dc22   2010003661

Editorial Credits
Kathryn Clay, editor; Tracy Davies, designer; Svetlana Zhurkin, media researcher;
    Laura Manthe, production specialist

Photo Credits
Alamy/ImageState, 22; The Bridgeman Art Library/Peter Newark Military Pictures/Private
Collection, 23; Commonwealth Air Training Plan Museum, 6; Corbis, 12; Corbis/Hulton-Deutsch
Collection, 17, 21; Courtesy of Harry S. Truman Library, 26 (top); Courtesy of Harry S. Truman
Library/U.S. Army Signal Corps, 28; DVIC/NARA, 25; Getty Images/Apic, 24; Getty Images
Keystone, cover (top), 9; Getty Images Keystone Features, 7; Getty Images Keystone/Horace
Abrahams, 26–27; Getty Images Popperfoto Paul Popper, 18; Getty Images/Roger Viollet, 11,
19; Getty Images/Time & Life Pictures U.S. Army Air Force, 14; iStockphoto/Duncan
Walker (Japanese naval ensign), cover; iStockphoto/John Cairns (helmet and gun), cover;
iStockphoto/Kris Hanke (smoke), cover, back cover, 1; iStockphoto/Linda Steward (letter),
cover; iStockphoto/Steve Christensen (barbed wire), cover; Library of Congress, 13, 15; Map
Resources, 5 (inset, left); NARA, 10; Shutterstock/Adam Tinney (flames), cover, back cover,
1; Shutterstock Ann Triling (stars), throughout; Shutterstock/Cagri Oner (torn paper),
throughout; Shutterstock/Igorsky (stone wall), 17, 21, 25; Shutterstock/kzww (rusty background),
throughout; Shutterstock/Lora Liu (paper background), throughout; XNR Productions (map), 5

Printed in the United States of America in Stevens Point, Wisconsin.
042011   006181R

TABLE OF CONTENTS

A WORLD DIVIDED

During the early 1930s, Adolf Hitler and his **Nazi** party rose to power in Germany. Hitler promised cheaper food and more jobs. He blamed other people, like Jews, for Germany's troubles. He declared that Germany should rule Europe.

By 1939, the heavy stomps of soldiers' boots echoed throughout Europe. Within three years, the Netherlands, Poland, France, Norway, and Denmark were all conquered by Germany. On the other side of the world, Japan invaded nearby China.

Germany, Japan, and Italy joined together as the main **Axis powers**. They were determined to rule the whole world. Great Britain, the Soviet Union, and several other countries became **Allied powers** who struggled to stop them. After Japan bombed Hawaii in December 1941, the United States joined the Allies.

Bloody battles raged everywhere. Tanks rumbled through Europe. Allied bombing raids turned cities into ruins. German submarines lurking in the Atlantic Ocean threatened North America.

Nazi: a member of a political party led by Adolf Hitler; Nazis ruled Germany from 1933 to 1945

Millions of men and women on both sides fought hard and died during World War II. Many soldiers suffered losses of legs or arms, wounds that changed their lives forever. Others never recovered from the horrible scenes they witnessed. Survivors' stories of heartbreak and courage live on years later.

Axis powers: a group of countries that fought together in World War II; the Axis powers included Japan, Italy, and Germany

Allied powers: a group of countries that fought together in World War II; some of the Allies were the United States, Canada, Great Britain, France, and the Soviet Union

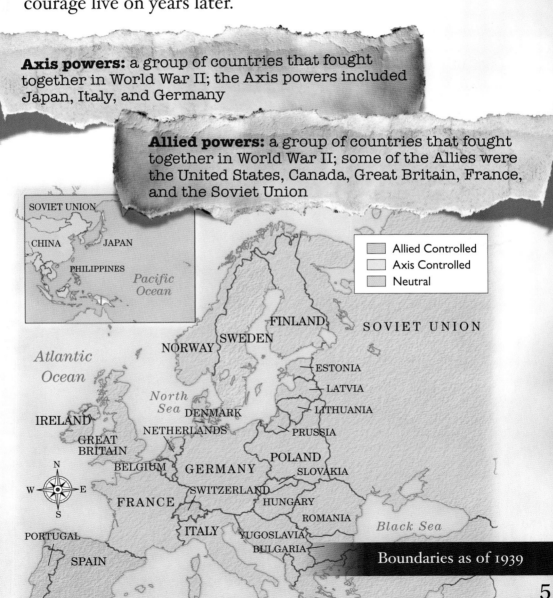

SOVIET UNION

CHINA   JAPAN

PHILIPPINES   *Pacific Ocean*

Allied Controlled
Axis Controlled
Neutral

FINLAND   SOVIET UNION
SWEDEN
NORWAY

Atlantic Ocean

ESTONIA
LATVIA
LITHUANIA

North Sea   DENMARK
IRELAND   PRUSSIA
NETHERLANDS
GREAT BRITAIN   POLAND
BELGIUM   GERMANY   SLOVAKIA
SWITZERLAND
FRANCE   HUNGARY
ROMANIA   *Black Sea*
PORTUGAL   ITALY   YUGOSLAVIA
BULGARIA
SPAIN

Boundaries as of 1939

2 WILLIAM ASH: BRITISH ESCAPE ARTIST

Pilot William Ash chewed his slice of bread and boiled cabbage. As after every meal in the German prison camp, he was still hungry. Like the other prisoners, he was thin and often sick. Ash had been shot down in his plane over France in March 1942. He was determined to escape from his German-run prison. He had tried several times since March without success. This time he had a really good plan.

Ash nodded to the men sitting at his table. One by one, they got up and walked across the cold ground to their **barracks**. Then they slipped out the back into a building full of toilets. The prisoners were digging a tunnel to freedom under a toilet. Their tunnel aimed toward a fence 150 feet (46 meters) away.

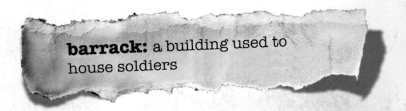

barrack: a building used to house soldiers

Lifting off the toilet, Ash lowered himself through the floor. He and the other prisoners always stripped naked before digging. If the guards saw the prisoners' filthy clothing, they would surely suspect something. They didn't seem to notice the horrible smell of the prisoners' bodies.

Above the tunnel, prisoners stomped on the ground to help hide the digging sounds. The Germans had placed microphones in the ground to listen for digging.

inside a barrack holding prisoners of war

Ash picked up a tin-can scoop with a wooden handle. He crawled through the tunnel, and the others followed. One man pumped air into the tunnel while they worked. Ash lit small candles made of boot laces smeared with margarine. As the men dug, they passed the dirt to others behind them. These men dumped the dirt into the waste pit. When the diggers were finished with their shift, they wriggled out of the tunnel. Eight more prisoners took their place.

THE ESCAPE

On March 5, 1943, 33 men squeezed into the tunnel. The men carried fake documents, civilian clothes, maps, and compasses that other prisoners had given them.

When the prisoners made it out, Ash said they "gasped and gulped in great lungfuls of fresh air." Then they ran in all directions. Unfortunately, Ash was captured within a week. Of the men who escaped, all but two were caught.

As Ash sat in his cell, he began planning his next escape. He succeeded during the last weeks of the war. While marching to a new prison, he snuck away and made it to British lines. They welcomed him as a hero.

A German WWII soldier guards prisoners.

RUTH STRAUB: AMERICAN ARMY NURSE

a U.S. army nurse

American army nurse Ruth Straub jumped off the rescue boat at Corregidor Island in the Philippines. The skies above were filled with Japanese bomber planes. Straub and the other nurses ran up a hill and threw themselves inside a huge tunnel. The nurses were tired, dirty, and wounded, but they had a job to do. Inside the tunnel was a hospital, and patients were waiting to be treated.

Straub had gone to the Philippines to help injured American soldiers. But Japanese pilots later bombed the hospital where Straub worked. The nurses and patients were then moved to Bataan Peninsula.

Patient beds in Bataan sat in open-air jungles among snakes and rats. No one could escape the terrible heat. The dust choked everyone. Earaches and headaches were common.

Japanese bombers flew overhead each day. The tunnel walls of the army hospital shook, and bottles fell off shelves. Straub and the other nurses dove under beds when the bombs came too close.

Japanese bombers

ORDERS TO LEAVE

Just before Japanese soldiers invaded the hospital, many of the nurses were ordered to leave. On May 4, 1942, Straub was among 13 nurses who climbed aboard a boat in the dark. They hated to leave behind their patients and fellow nurses. But they were relieved to escape the horror. A few miles offshore, a huge shape surfaced. It was the submarine USS *Spearfish*. The nurses slipped through a hatch and into the sub. Minutes later, the sub disappeared underwater.

Life was crowded on the sub. Straub breathed stale air and suffered from the heat. Straub and the other nurses helped cook, serve meals, and wash dishes. By the third week of May, the submarine made it to Australia. Straub was shipped home soon after.

When submarines weren't transporting nurses and soldiers, they patrolled the Pacific Ocean.

JUST IN TIME

Straub had boarded the submarine just in time. On May 11, Japanese soldiers overran the hospital. The nurses who had stayed behind were held in a prison camp in Manila, Philippines, until 1945.

Nurses wore helmets similar to those used by soldiers.

4 DAVID WEBSTER: AMERICAN PARATROOPER

a U.S. paratrooper

David Webster pulled on long underwear, trousers, a shirt, and a jumpsuit. He clipped on his **bayonet**, knife, and first-aid kit. With more than 100 pounds (45 kilograms) of equipment, he was weighed down like a knight in stiff armor. The heavy weight made it difficult for Webster to breathe in the summer heat. But it was D-Day, and he was ready to fight.

Webster and his fellow paratroopers climbed inside a dark plane. They sat on metal bucket seats. As the plane flew over the English Channel, Webster saw a huge fleet of ships stretched out for miles. Barges, destroyers, cruisers, and transports carried thousands of troops. He thought they looked "like a flood of lava."

bayonet: a long metal blade attached to the end of a musket or rifle

THE BIG JUMP

The plane dove up and down, zigzagging to avoid enemy fire. Webster was thrown from side to side. The plane smelled like a mix of smoke, oil, and vomit. The stench made Webster gag. As they neared the drop point, the men checked one another's equipment. Then they moved toward the open door. Everyone seemed ready to get the jump over with. As Webster jumped, he was puzzled to see only water below. When his parachute opened, his body swung hard in the wind. He landed feetfirst in water up to his hips.

Webster threw off his parachute and pulled out his rifle. Bullets from German machine guns splashed in the water around him. He crouched as he loaded his rifle and pulled out his compass. When he saw that the water had destroyed his compass, he tossed it away. He couldn't see any of the landmarks he'd been trained to look for. Where was he?

paratroopers preparing to jump

15

A LONG JOURNEY AHEAD

Webster threw away his gas mask and hand grenades to lighten his load. Then he heard the swish of water. Someone was coming. He grabbed his clicker, a child's toy given to each soldier to use as a signal. With one hand on his gun's trigger, Webster clicked the toy. Just as he was ready to shoot, he heard another click. He put away his gun and welcomed a fellow American soldier.

When the moon came out from behind clouds, Webster and his new partner could see hills. As they headed toward the hills, they met more American soldiers. Webster insisted they keep looking for the rest of the soldiers. He took off his wet shirt and pants, rolled up his soaked underwear, and put his jumpsuit back on. As he marched away, Webster heard the others follow.

The soldiers crossed wet ditches holding their rifles high above their heads to keep them dry. When they finally made it up a steep hill, the soldiers sat gasping for air. After the sun rose, they snuck through a forest and found the rest of their unit in a nearby village. Now they were ready to march toward Germany.

Hundreds of paratroopers dropped over France on D-Day.

The Allies Invade Europe

Webster parachuted into Normandy, France, on June 6, 1944. This day is now known as D-Day. The Allies chose Normandy as the place to begin an all-out effort to defeat Germany and end the war. Normandy was close enough to Great Britain that Allied planes could help protect the soldiers who landed there. Less than a year after D-Day, Germany surrendered.

HANNA REITSCH: NAZI PILOT

Hanna Reitsch was the best test pilot in Germany. Because of her skills with gliders and airplanes, Hitler had awarded her Germany's top medals. She was also offered a place in the air force. But Reitsch didn't want to be ordered around. She turned down the offer.

In April 1945, Hitler chose General Robert von Greim as his new air force commander. The general was told to join Hitler in Berlin. But Berlin was surrounded by enemy troops. Flying in or out would be almost impossible.

Even though he didn't know the way, the new commander insisted on flying the plane himself. Reitsch worried that von Greim wouldn't be able to handle the problems awaiting him. She volunteered to ride along. Before taking off, Reitsch made sure she could reach the controls if needed.

FLYING TO BERLIN

As they neared Berlin, the plane was hit by enemy fire. Both engines flamed as von Greim slumped in his seat. He had been shot and could no longer fly the plane. Reitsch grabbed the controls and turned the plane to avoid gunfire. She couldn't see landmarks through the smoke. But she could see gasoline pouring out of both wing tanks. Soon the plane would have no power. She remembered a famous Berlin tower. She headed there and landed just as the plane ran out of gas.

German fighter planes

HITLER'S BUNKER

Reitsch and von Greim waited on the side of the road to be picked up. Luckily, Germans found them before the enemy did. They rode through a city of burned wreckage, rubble, and thick smoke to Hitler's **bunker**. Reitsch couldn't sleep the first night in the bunker. Even though she was 50 feet (15 meters) underground, constant gunfire overhead kept her awake. Hitler and his advisors still hoped for a German victory. Reitsch knew this was impossible.

LEAVING BERLIN

On April 29, 1945, Reitsch and von Greim once again traveled through the flaming city. They found a plane in an airfield still controlled by the Germans. The plane's pilot flew them safely out of Berlin. Shortly afterward, Germany surrendered to the Allies, ending the war. For her participation in the war, Reitsch spent 15 months in prison. When she was released, she continued to fly.

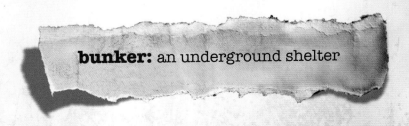

bunker: an underground shelter

In March 1941, Hitler presented Reitsch with the Iron Cross medal.

Hitler's Last Day

Hitler refused to be captured by the Allies. On April 30, 1945, he shot himself. Some of his top advisors committed suicide as well. Other advisors were captured and put on trial for war crimes.

6 HAYASHI ICHIZO: JAPANESE KAMIKAZE PILOT

a Japanese pilot

By 1945, the Japanese were desperate. Hoping to frighten their enemies, air force commanders ordered pilots to join a special unit. The men in this unit were called **kamikazes**. These men were instructed to fly their planes directly into enemy ships. The planes would be destroyed, and the pilots would die for their country.

On February 22, 1945, 22-year-old Hayashi Ichizo received his orders. Many kamikaze pilots were proud to sacrifice their lives for their country. But Ichizo dreaded the task ahead of him. He said, "To be honest, I cannot say that the wish to die for the emperor is genuine."

"To be honest, I cannot say that the wish to die for the emperor is genuine."

kamikaze: a member of a Japanese air attack corps in World War II who would purposely crash his plane into a target, resulting in his own death

a Japanese kamikaze attack on a U.S. aircraft carrier

A DEADLY MISSION

Ichizo's mission was scheduled for March 21 but was delayed because of airplane problems. Half of his friends did fly that day. They dove their planes into enemy vessels off the Japanese island of Okinawa.

When his turn came, Ichizo put on a headband showing the rising sun. He wore a white scarf around his neck. These were symbols of Japan and the kamikaze squads. To Ichizo, the whole thing felt like a dream. He promised he would sing as he flew. On April 12, Ichizo took off with other kamikaze pilots. None of the pilots returned.

a Japanese kamikaze putting on his headband

A mushroom cloud rose over Nagasaki after the atomic bomb was dropped.

Ending the War

When Japan refused to surrender, the United States decided to do something extreme. In August 1945, the United States dropped two atomic bombs on the Japanese cities Hiroshima and Nagasaki. Each bomb blasted twice the amount of heat needed to melt iron. In Hiroshima, more than 100,000 people died from radiation. The bombings left the Japanese with few options. On August 14, they surrendered to the Allies.

7 THE COST OF WAR

Tokyo in ruins after the war

Between 60 and 65 million soldiers and civilians were killed in World War II. Homes, bridges, factories, and churches lay in ruins. The U.S. government sent money to both its allies and former enemies to help with the rebuilding. It also provided medical care for Japanese who suffered from the atomic bomb attacks.

While marching across Europe, Allied troops were shocked to see the Nazi concentration camps. The camps were filled with starving Jews and captured soldiers. While these prisoners were rescued, others were not so lucky. More than six million Jewish people were killed at these camps during the war.

Leaders of the Axis powers were brought to trial. They were charged with using slave labor, setting up death camps, and torturing soldiers and civilians. For their crimes, some Axis leaders were given prison sentences. Others were put to death.

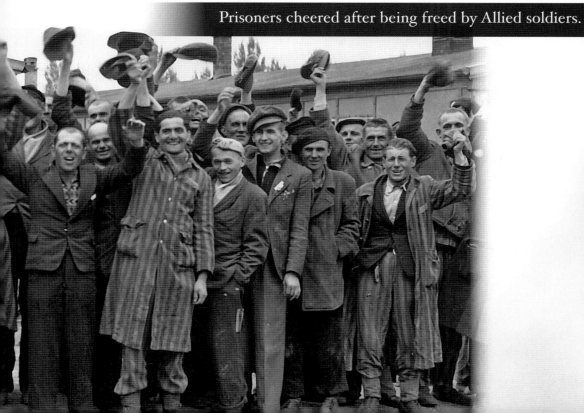

Prisoners cheered after being freed by Allied soldiers.

The destruction caused during World War II was devastating. Entire cities were destroyed. Anger between nations caused unrest. Millions of lives were lost. But since the war's end more than 60 years ago, nations have worked together. They want to prevent this type of worldwide destruction from ever happening again.

British Prime Minister Winston Churchill, U.S. President Harry S. Truman, and Soviet leader Josef Stalin (left to right) met after the war to create peace treaties.

GLOSSARY

Allied powers (AL-lyd POU-urs)—a group of countries that fought together in World War II; some of the Allies were the United States, Canada, Great Britain, and France

atomic bomb (uh-TAH-mik BOM)—a powerful explosive that destroys large areas; atomic bombs leave behind harmful elements called radiation

Axis powers (AK-siss POU-urs)—a group of countries that fought together in World War II; the Axis powers included Japan, Italy, and Germany

barrack (BEAR-uhk)—a building used to house soldiers

bayonet (BAY-uh-net)—a long metal blade attached to the end of a musket or rifle

bunker (BUHNGK-ur)—an underground shelter

civilian (si-VIL-yuhn)—a person who is not in the military

fleet (FLEET)—a group of ships

kamikaze (kah-mi-KAH-zee)—a member of a Japanese air attack corps in World War II who would purposely crash his plane into a target, resulting in his own death

Nazi (NOT-see)—a member of a political party led by Adolf Hitler; Nazis ruled Germany from 1933 to 1945

BIBLIOGRAPHY

Ash, William with Brendan Foley. *Under the Wire: the World War II Adventures of a Legendary Escape Artist and Cooler King*. New York: Thomas Dunn Books/St. Martin's Press, 2005.

Norman, Elizabeth M. *We Band of Angels: The Untold Story of American Nurses Trapped on Bataan by the Japanese*. New York: Random House, 1999.

Ohnuki-Tierney, Emiko. *Kamikaze Diaries: Reflections of Japanese Student Soldiers*. Chicago: University of Chicago Press, 2006.

Reitsch, Hanna. *Flying Is My Life*. Translated by Lawrence Wilson. New York: Putnam, 1954.

Webster, David Kenyon. *Parachute Infantry: An American Paratrooper's Memoir of D-Day and the Fall of the Third Reich*. New York: Delta Trade Paperbacks, 2002.

READ MORE

Conway, John Richard. *Primary Source Accounts of World War II*. America's Wars Through Primary Sources. Berkeley Heights, N.J.: MyReportLinks.com Books, 2006.

Miller, Terry. *D-Day: The Allies Strike Back During World War II*. 24/7 Goes to War. New York: Franklin Watts, 2010.

Raum, Elizabeth. *World War II: An Interactive History Adventure*. You Choose Books. Mankato, Minn.: Capstone Press, 2009.

INTERNET SITES

FactHound offers a safe, fun way to find Internet sites related to this book. All of the sites on FactHound have been researched by our staff.

Here's all you do:

Visit *www.facthound.com*

Type in this code: 9781429647380

INDEX